Donald Tolmie Masson

Vestigia Celtica

Celtic Footprints in Philology, Ethics and Religion

Donald Tolmie Masson

Vestigia Celtica
Celtic Footprints in Philology, Ethics and Religion

ISBN/EAN: 9783337296018

Printed in Europe, USA, Canada, Australia, Japan

Cover: Foto ©Thomas Meinert / pixelio.de

More available books at **www.hansebooks.com**

Celtic Footprints

IN

Philology, Ethics, and Religion.

BY

DONALD MASSON,

M.A., M.D.

———◆———

EDINBURGH : MACLACHLAN AND STEWART.
LONDON: TRÜBNER AND CO.
DUBLIN: M. H. GILL AND SON.
1882.

EDINBURGH: PRINTED BY NEILL AND COMPANY,
GOVERNMENT BOOK AND LAW PRINTERS FOR SCOTLAND.

```
*   *   *
 *   *   *
  *   *
   *
```

THIS little volume, though complete in
itself, so far as it goes, is offered to my
countrymen as the first part of a much
larger work, the materials of which I have
been preparing for some years. Thus far
I have but opened the quarry, and, with
the first stones taken therefrom, have
built a chapel, which may, I hope, here-
after form the chancel of a well-propor-
tioned church.

That hope may, or may not, be fulfilled.
For it rests with my countrymen to say
whether or not I shall proceed with the
work, and complete the edifice which I
have designed. These chapters are pub-
lished at my own expense. Whether or
not there shall be more to follow, depends

mainly on the encouragement which is vouchsafed to the present venture.

Small though this work is, it is the fruit of no small labour in the way of antecedent preparatory research. That labour has been its own rich reward, and it has been lightened too by the helping hand of friends. I am thus greatly indebted to Professor Eggeling, the learned professor of Sanskrit and Comparative Philology in the University of Edinburgh, and to my young friend, and former pupil in Gaelic, Mr. Thomas Cockburn, M.A., a linguist of rare ability and promise. I owe much also to Mr. Small and Mr. Clarke, the respective and much respected chiefs of the University and Advocates' Libraries. But most of all am I indebted to the authorities of the great National Library of France, the vast resources of whose unrivalled collections were on several occasions freely thrown open to me. My warm acknowledgments are also due to the Rev. Charles Maceachern, whose practical knowledge of printing, and whose familiarity with the peculiarities of the Gaelic spoken in Islay and Tiree, have been most useful to me.

But for the serious expense of materially altering the proof-sheets, I would have recast and amplified some of the sentences on pp. 20, 21 ; and I would have introduced a new paragraph, containing illustrations from the Old Irish, at p. 25. As it is, however, I can here but refer the reader, for further elucidation of the points there dealt with, to the sixth of Max Müller's *Lectures on the Science of Language,* and to Chapter VI. of Windisch's *Kurzgefasste Irische Grammatik.*

My mode of Gaelic scription will, I know, give grave offence to some critics. I can't help it. For the life of me, I cannot see that any good end is to be served by our continuing any longer to speckle the pages of our Gaelic books all over with a barbarous garniture of accent and inverted comma. Like warts and patches on the face of a court beauty, this barbarous practice was once regarded as

a wonderful embellishment. To the Eliza-
bethan printer of English it was as dear as
it is to-day to our purists in the mint and
cummin of Celtic scholarship. But no
printer of English out of Bedlam would
now dream of returning to a practice so
rude and disfiguring. And why should
not we too have the courage to dismiss it
to the limbo of technical superstitions ?
The practice is not only in itself an un-
seemly disfigurement of our Gaelic books.
It tends to repel, on the threshold of their
first attempt, many who, but for it, would
learn to read in Gaelic ; and its fancied
difficulties have prevented many a Highlander of promising parts from ever
attempting to commit to writing, in his
mother tongue, thoughts which otherwise
might have greatly enriched the literature
of the Gael.

CONTENTS.

CHAPTER I.

CHAPTER II.

CHAPTER III.

CHAPTER IV.

CHAPTER V.

CHAPTER VI.

CHAPTER VII.

CHAPTER VIII.

CHAPTER IX.

CHAPTER I.

INTRODUCTORY.

In the hands of the scientific philologist the language of the Gael has already furnished definite results, whose value and volume it were not easy to exaggerate. The large vocabulary which the merest tyro in British philology can now identify as common to Irish, Scotch Gaelic, and Manx, has been shown by the application of a few simple, well-proved laws of letter-change, to be also largely identical with the living speech of Wales and Brittany, and with the language but lately spoken in Cornwall. Its close connection, also, is no longer problematical with that language, long dead and buried from view, whose

A

precious remains, not less time-worn and weather-wasted on the stone than in substance blurred and obscured by the linguistic change of sixteen centuries, are now being patiently deciphered from the old Gaulish inscriptions. And of what is thus shown to belong to the whole Celtic family much has been similarly proved to be indeed the common patrimony of the great Aryan race. By a process seeming almost to combine the delicate manipulation of the picture-restorer with the keen disciplined intuition and "scientific imagination" of the practised palæontologist, the student of language has constructed, out of materials largely Celtic, a great science of Word-History, not unworthy to be compared with that science which treats of the Life of the Globe, extant and extinct, animal and vegetable.

In this field of mere Word-History the labours of the great workers on the Continent, who may be said to have first founded a school of rational Celtic philology, and the researches of their later and more

favoured disciples in Britain, such as Stokes
and Rhys, have left little to be done, at
least in the way of original research, by
the Celtic scholars of the rising generation.

In the fresher fields of Grammatical
Inflection—the history and linguistic significance of case-endings and verb-modifica-
tions—while undoubtedly much good work
has already been done, especially by Ebel
and Windisch, there yet remains an abund-
ance of untouched virgin ore, with not a
little of much belaboured but, I think, still
richly auriferous " dirt," which to the im-
proved tests and methods of future philo-
logists may prove a veritable California.
But great preliminary difficulties must be
removed, and some missing links must be
recovered, ere the goodly harvest of our
expectations can be gathered from this
field into the garner of Inflectional Philology.

One field, however, of Celtic philology
may still be said to lie all unbroken ; a field,
the intelligent cultivation of whose virgin
soil must, one would think, in the order of

Nature, precede any satisfactory culture of the further field of Grammatical Inflection. Between us and this distal field of grammatical inflection, the philological instinct, it appears to me, has always been feeling for a proximal field of less enigmatical research; a field in turning over whose less tenacious furrows one might expect to light on some fragments of linguistic pottery, which, pieced together, might form the perfect moulds of inflectional forms now so time-worn as to be unintelligible. And if ever this hypothetical home-field of philology is to become a fertile reality, I confidently expect that it will be found, not in any dead language like the highly elaborated Sanskrit, but in the rude, unelaborated forms of the living Celtic. Nay, I propose now to show that in the current Scotch Gaelic of the Highlands such a field is already open to the philologist, and that too in a state, not merely of wonderful preservation, but of singular freshness and rich recuperative vitality. What is here pointed at, be it observed, is not the old

well-gleaned, well-trodden field of mere
verbal linguistics, but a new field in Celtic
philology, of what may be called Rudimen-
tary Sentence-building; a field whereon,
as it appears to me, may be investigated
the earliest attempts at the process by
which the pattern of human thought—
ethical, social, and religious—is first rudely
shaped out to the mind's eye of hearer or
reader, and in some measure to the speaker's
own clearer consciousness, by the warp and
woof of woven words. On this field, I
believe, it is that the Gaelic language will
prove most truly interesting in itself, and
most largely helpful to the student of
philology. For that language, with all the
elasticity of a living, plastic organism, ex-
hibits a wondrous wealth of such rudely
elementary expedients, for expressing grammatical relations, as may well be taken for
Nature's earliest germinal efforts at word-
weaving into the significant pattern of
intelligible statement or proposition. The
form of these rude linguistic contrivances
still used in Gaelic is infinitely various.

But underlying this infinite variety of form there is one definite dominating idea, presently to be illustrated. That underlying idea is undoubtedly of high linguistic antiquity. Some little knowledge of languages so far apart as Sanskrit and Archaic French, as well as my special reading in the Celtic tongues, has enabled me to trace its analogue, more or less obvious, along the whole front of that wide linguistic gamut. The common mother of the Gadhelic and Cymric families of speech must have used it; for all her living descendants—Gaelic, Irish, Breton, and to some extent Welsh— use it to this day; as did also the Cornish to the last. As a linguistic fossil, in various stages of development or degradation, and very variously preserved, it is firmly bedded in the substance of every language that I know. But in the living Gaelic it displays, in wondrous volume and variety, all the plastic vitality of a living organism. And what now is the philological significance of this fact? That I may overrate the value of what I am about to lay before the

reader is not at all impossible. But yet I
venture, in all soberness of mind, to submit
that it furnishes, out of the living present,
much that may help us to understand, and
mayhap rehabilitate, the dead exuviæ of the
past. As in the teeming forms of lower
life the biologist finds the analogues of
man's fœtal growth and development, so
may the student of language, through the
living speech of the Highlander, here study,
as it were, at once the embryology and
morphology of Language in general, and so
expect to extend and greatly to fertilise
the whole domain of philology.

And be it remembered that whatever
thus helps us to decipher the ancient coin-
forms of human expression, in word, phrase,
idiom, or inflection, affords also a suggestion, at the least, for estimating their primitive money's worth in human thought.

The wide field here opened up to view
is not only of great extent, but it presents
to us a great variety of aspects. Within
the limits of these chapters I can attempt
to explore of that wide field but one definite

section. Even if my space were more
abundant, it were better, perhaps, to defer
consideration of the wider inquiry, until
what is now to be advanced shall have
been sifted and tested by criticism. My
materials have, moreover, grown so much
under my hands, that except in laying the
main foundations of my thesis, I must for
the present pass over many parallel usages
in Breton, Cornish, and Welsh, and con-
fine my illustrations mainly to the narrower
ground of Irish and Manx.

CHAPTER II.

THE FUNDAMENTAL PRINCIPLE.

OF all those rude Gaelic expedients, still so largely used to express the grammatical relations of words in a sentence, I shall begin with one which, without being particularly striking, has the advantage of being simple. Notably conspicuous in Gaelic, it has moreover the further advantage, for the purpose in hand, of being still to some extent traceable in almost every other language with which I am acquainted. And, as will appear farther on, it is the mother-form of a vast and varied linguistic progeny. This is the simple expedient whereby, in Gaelic, we indicate which one, of two or more objects in the same sentence, we regard as, for the moment, the most prominent or important. And how does the Gael attain this object of expressing relative degrees of demonstrative emphasis? By the natural device of what may be called the Verbal Perspective of Sentence-building : *i.e., by identifying the Prominence of an object with its local Proximity to the speaker.* In grouping his word-picture the Gael does, as if by primitive natural instinct, what the painter does by the teaching of his divine art; he groups his materials according to his sense of what, to himself as the centre, should be their relative local proximity.

Now, is it too much to hazard here the conjecture that in this the Gael continues, down to the present day, to do as we may well suppose men to have done in their first rude attempts to construct a sentence? What, for the time, is most important to me I keep nearest me; it may be that there I may the better protect it; it may be that there it may the better protect, or otherwise serve me. When this preference

on my part ceases, the object loses its pre-
eminence; yielding up its place of prior
interest and consequent proximity to some
other object, now nearer to my thoughts.
This instinctive adjustment of the relative
local position of the elements of primitive
" speech-matter " grows, gradually and
naturally, into the grammatical *idea* of a
local, or "space," relation between the
word-members of a statement or proposition. That idea of "space" relation may
long be of very limited scope and application. It may, indeed, be acted upon as an
unconscious instinct, long before it is consciously realised, or at all clearly evolved
as an idea. But potentially it is already
paramount; is, in fact, the potential mother-
thought of all grammatical relations, and of
the conscious notional distinctions to which
these grammatical distinctions give expression. The germ, the nucleated mother-cell,
if one may so speak, is there already,
waiting to be fertilised, with the widening
of my experience, acquisitions, and growing
wants and desires, for the production, *pro*

re nata, of all the more complex grammatical relations of disciplined thinking, and of the perfected speech of educated men. We know that the Locative case is ideally the most primitive, some hold that actually it is the oldest, of all Indo-European case-endings. Even so does this idea of the relations of things *in space* thus gradually extend its scope, till it embraces and regulates our grammatical contrivances for expressing all possible relations of things to one another. Nay, this idea of the relations of *things* in *space* grows gradually into some dawning conception of the relation of *deeds* in *time*. And so, in due time, are evolved from this small beginning the endless forms of various self-modifying relations, arising out of my multiplying environments—material, social, and moral —as in my own person doing, owning, accumulating, suffering, giving and receiving, influenced and influencing, in the multiform exchange of civilised human life.

M. Salomon Reinach, in his *Manual de Philologie*, p. 144, goes so far as confidently to assert that the Demonstrative Pronouns in all Indo-European languages, are formed from *ta*, *i*, and *ya*. He holds, moreover, that all true prepositions can be referred to a pronominal origin. The former statement M. Reinach, in a courteous letter with which he has favoured me, frankly admits to be " too absolute," and he informs me of his intention to modify it in the forthcoming new edition of his very learned work. Adding *sa* and *a*, however, these two statements of M. Reinach's may be taken as, in the main, not very far from the truth. And it was while endeavouring, in a tentative way, to test the theory which they enunciate, and to fill up its numerous lacunæ with materials drawn from the rich and varied intercompoundings, in Gaelic, of Preposition and Pronoun, that my attention was first engaged in the linguistic significance of the facts now to be set forth.

At first, however, I shall, for the sake of simplicity, deal with the linguistic affinities, not at all of Pronoun and Preposition, but only of the Pronouns Demonstrative and Adverbs of Place. In Gaelic the equivalents of *This* and *Here*, of *That* and *There*, of *Yon* and *Yonder*, are respectively identical. Thus, *an leabhar so* is *the book here*, or *this book; an leabhar sin* is *the book there*, or *that book;* and *an leabhar (s)ud* is, as we say in Scotland, *yon book* (*that farther book*), or *the book yonder*. All through the Gaelic language the Pronouns Demonstrative are similarly identical with the corresponding Adverbs of Place. Nor is it otherwise in Irish and the other kindred tongues.

That herein, as practically speaking in all else of the least significance to the philologist, the Irish should be at one with the Gaelic, goes indeed without saying. Ever since the mission of Columba, and probably for centuries before it, there was a constant interchange of thought, and there was frequent intercourse of men, between old and new Scotia. And, indeed, till the beginning of the present century, the only Gaelic Bible we had in Scotland was either Bedell's Irish translation, in the Irish

character, or Kirk's transliteration of Bedell into Roman type, for the use of Scottish
Highlanders. The latter was first printed
in 1690, and was twice afterwards reprinted,
before we had in Scotland a Gaelic Bible
of our own.

Nor is there really any great difference
in this respect between Gaelic and Manx.
The printed page of the Manx Bible does,
indeed, present to the eye an appearance,
differing in a marked degree from a page
of printed Gaelic. But it is a difference of
orthographic form, rather than of verbal
substance ; a difference, too, which can very
easily be explained. The Manx translators
wrote their language phonetically. After
careful consideration, they came to the
conclusion that, to be understood by the
common people, for whom mainly they
wrote, their Manx translation of the Scriptures must spell out its words as the Manx
people of that time pronounced them. They
came to this conclusion with regret ; for in
acting upon it they felt that they sacrificed
much in regard to " the etymology of

words," and " the connection between roots
and compounds," as well as a noble oppor-
tunity, as they thought, of restoring the
language to " its original energy and
purity" (Gill's *Introduction to Kelly's
Manx Grammar*, p. 13). Making allow-
ance, then, for the different principles of
scription, it will be seen that Gaelic, Irish,
and Manx are really but one language in
all that concerns this identity of the demonstrative pronouns with the corresponding
adverbs of place; thus, *am fear so* = (Irish)
an fear so = (Manx) yn fer shoh = at once,
this man and *the* man here; *am fear sin* =
an fear sin = yn fer shen = *that man* and
the man there; am fear (s)ud = an fear sud
= yn fer shid = *yonder man* and *the man
yonder*.

The Welsh does not greatly differ, *e.g.*,
y dyn yma = both *this man* and *the man
here;* and *y dyn acw* = *that man* and *the
man there.* I am not aware of a parallel
in Welsh for the third example in the
paragraph immediately preceding.

In Cornish *hem, hemma* = this; *an rem-*

ma, an re hemma = these ; *omma* = here. In composition *hemma* and *omma* are contracted into 'ma ; as *am blyven-ma*, this pen ; *an leavar-ma*, this book. Or the suffix *'ma* may be added without the hyphen ; as *am byzma*, this world ; *an ulazma*, this country. So also *hen, henna* = *that* and *there*, appearing with the noun as the suffix *'na*. Thus *an manu-na*, that boy ; *a guaz-na*, that fellow ; *en kuz-na*, that wood ; *en ur-na*, then, at that hour.

In Breton the identity of adverbs of place with the demonstrative pronouns is almost as clearly obvious as in Gaelic. Thus *aman* = here (ici) ; *aze* = there (là-près) ; and *ahont* = yonder (là-loin). Corresponding to this we find *ar bugel ma*, or *man* = this boy ; *ann den-ze* = that man ; *ar vioc'h-hont* = yonder cow.

Instances of a similar usage in the non-Celtic tongues must for the present be regarded as lying outside the plan of these chapters.

Now, from the linguistic point of view, what have we here? I figure to myself

B

an ancient Celt in the far prehistoric times.
He sits by a heap of rough 'nodular flint
stones, such as one sees to-day in the chalk
pits and railway-cuttings near Brighton.
To supply himself with some needful tool
or weapon, he splits the oblong nodular
flint-stones into flakes—splits them perhaps
with the same ease and skill, perhaps with
as light a tap of his rude hammer, though
it be not yet of metal, as does the patient
flint-dresser of to-day, when preparing
material for that outer encasement of shining flint, which gives to the old churches
of Sussex their peculiar charm of architec-
ture. Three flakes of shining flint stand
out conspicuous in the little heap, which
forms his open-air factory—to him all that
the great forges of Armstrong and Whit-
worth are to us. Of the three flakes of
flint he chooses one, as best fitted for his
purpose. Taking it up, it becomes to him
the flint *here;* the other flints, so far as for
the moment they concern him, being *there,*
yonder, or *nowhere*. His flint *here* we call
this one, his flint *there* we call *that* one, the

farther flint we call *you* one. But to him *this*, *that*, and *you* flints are still the flint *here* beside him, the flint *there* before him, the flint *farther away*, which is beyond him. The *local* relation is either the one relation of his conceptions, or the one relation whose practical importance to him deserves a name. And down to this day the language he spoke, through all its changes, makes no distinction between its idea of the local proximity of objects and the more complex idea of their relative importance. In the illustrations just given, I have purposely introduced the English words *before*, *beside*, and *beyond*. These words, we know, were themselves at one time used in a sense exclusively local. But *before* has now, in great measure, lost its primitive signification of *locality*, and is mainly used to express relations of *time*; *beside*, in the altered form of *besides*, is mostly used to express relations of *comparative excess*, save in the ominous, but significant, case of a man being *beside himself*; while *beyond*, like its Breton equivalent *hont*, is still mainly used in a sense not *temporal* but *local*. The history of the English word *near* affords another very simple illustration of the same principle. Originally confined to the domain of *space*, it now deals also, not only with *time*, but with all the vicissitudes of *mind* and *fate*. The time, as I write, may be *near* the hour of dinner, or the chop *nearly* done to a turn. A man may be *near* death, or *nearly* blind, or *near* perfection, even as, by process of the same philological phenomenon, he may, in our living vernacular English, be *next-door* to a devil. The Breton word for *near*, still used in Bretagne as a preposition or adverb of place, bears to us in Scotch Gaelic a suggestion of somewhat similar significance. The Breton *tost*, near, French *près*, Latin *prope*, has for comparative *tostoc'h*, propius, and for the superlative *tosta*, proxime. The strength of the third consonant in *tost* will be, doubtless, to some an insuperable barrier to its alliance with the Old Gaelic *toiseach*, beginning, primus, princeps. None the less, however, may this Breton *tost* put in a fair claim of kinship, through the Old Gaelic *toiseach*, with the great Clan Mac-in-tosh!

As has been said, this passage of a relation at first simply local into relations higher, wider, and more complex, might be to some extent illustrated, though mostly in fossil forms, from well-nigh all the Indo-European languages. But in the Gadhelic tongues this principle of verbal perspective, grouping our words into significant sentences on the plan of relative local proximity, is still a living, plastic, formative organism. If the reader will turn to Windisch's *Kurzgefasste Irische Grammatik*, chap. vi., §§ 190-198, he will see that the same principle is as firmly rooted in the substance of the Old Irish speech as in the vernacular Gaelic of the modern Highlander. And in the next chapter I shall proceed to show how this principle directly inspires and dominates the whole field of Gadhelic phrase and idiom.

CHAPTER III.

To the student of social ethics that may
seem a transition not less immoral than far
fetched whereby *this* flint knife, kept here
beside me, becomes *my* knife, or *that* one,
farther away, may if you like, because it is
not so handy to me, become *thy* property,
or *yonder* one, still farther off, and indifferent to me and to you, may lie there and
become *his* property who may choose to
take it. The tie which would thus con-
stitute the connection of owner and property, however much it may resemble the

ethics of our own childhood, savours to the moralist too much of

> The good old rule,
>> The simple plan,
> That he shall take who has the might,
>> And he shall keep who can.

But to the mind and habits of the primitive Celt this transition seems to have been neither strange nor uncongenial. That such, indeed, was the case his speech still bewrayeth him. Thus, *an cu agam* (aig mi) = the dog at me = my dog; *an cu agad* (aig tu) = the dog at thee = thy dog; *an cu aige* (aig e) = the dog at him = his dog; *an cu aice* (aig i) = the dog at her = her dog; *an cu againn* (aig sinn) = the dog at us = our dog; *an cu agaibh* (aig sibh) = the dog at you = your dog; *an cu aca* (aig iad) = the dog at them = their dog. Similarly also we say *an cu aig Seumas* = the dog at James = James' dog.

In written Gaelic the idea of ownership is no doubt also expressed by using the genitive case of the owner, as *cu Sheumais* = James' dog. But in the ordinary colloquial speech of the Highland people, the form given above is that all but universally employed—the form, to wit, which makes that my property which is *at me, nearest me,* so long as I can, or choose to, keep it there.

If again, with the help of a verb, I make a distinct statement in regard to the holding of property, the same principle comes at once into play. Thus, *tha tigh agam* = is house at me = I have a house; *tha tigh agad* = is house at thee = thou hast a house; *tha tigh aige* = is house at him = he has a house; *tha tigh aig Seumas* = is house at James = James has a house.

And here I pray the reader to observe that to this analytic form there is in Gaelic no alternative synthetic form of speech, by means of which a definite statement, in regard to the holding of property, may be clearly and grammatically made. There is, indeed, speaking broadly, an alternative analytic form, by the use the preposition *le*, with, which shall be fully considered in a subsequent chapter. What here falls to be considered is that, when speaking generally about James' house, I can say either *tigh Sheumais*, or *an tigh aig Scumas*. But when making the distinct statement that James possesses a house, I can only say *tha tigh aig Seumas*. I call attention to this fact, because I wish here to anticipate a form of criticism which these chapters are not unlikely to provoke. It may fairly be asked whether the tendency indicated by the idiomatic usages here collected may not be a tendency the very reverse of what has been suggested—that is, a tendency from an original synthetic to a more modern analytic form of speech? Well, even if it were so, my critic must not forget that which is clearly implied in his hypothesis; for he must remember that the latter is only a repetition, on a different principle, of the former, after the loss of the old inflections. And he must especially remember what has just been shown in regard to the absence of any other way than the analytic of making, in Gaelic, a distinct statement as to the holding of property.

Were my acquaintance with the oldest remains of written Irish wider and more exact than it is, I might, possibly enough, find good cause to modify, or even to abandon, the position here taken up. But in the Old Irish texts which have been edited by Zeuss and by Stokes, as well as in authorities so excellent and accurate as Windisch's *Irische Texte* and his *Kurzge-fasste Irische Grammatik*, I have met with nothing to invalidate, but have found, on the contrary, a good deal to strengthen that position. On pp. 116, 117 of Windisch's work last named, no fewer than four examples of the idiom in question may readily be found, and two examples of it meet the eye on p. 121. Without quoting the sentences at length, I will take the two examples which can best be separated from the context : *ni acca nech acht Condla a o'enur*=he had none but Conn alone ; *mac sainmeal oc Nuadait*=Nuada's most distinguished son. See also Windisch's *Irische Texte*, in " Scél mucci Mic Dáthó," p. 96, *bui cu oca*=bha cu aige=he had a dog.

From Stokes' *Goidelica*, pp. 101, 103, take also these : *ni bói biad occu acht criathar corca* = they had no food but a sieveful of oats ; and *cris mobi occu* = they had Mobi's girdle. Several examples, too long to be here quoted, will be found in Zeuss' *Grammatica Celtica*, 2nd edition, pp. 634–636, under the preposition *oc*. One more illustration and I pass on. The grammar of the learned Windisch, above referred to, will readily be accepted as one of our latest and most trustworthy authorities on Old Irish. Now if the reader will turn to pp. 47, 48 of that work, he will find declined at full length, with the three pronominal suffixes, not only the preposition *oc*, in the sense assigned to it by me in this chapter, but also the other prepositions which remain to be similarly dealt with in the chapters yet to follow. And after that reference, the reader will probably agree with me that, in future chapters, his patience may be spared the task of struggling through a great many quotations from Old Irish authorities. What has been quoted above has been here introduced only to anticipate a line of criticism which might otherwise very fairly be taken up. It is of course conceded that no number of quotations, however large and apposite, can entirely obviate such criticism. But while frankly making that concession, I plead that I have here one good point, at least, honestly scored in my favour. I have shown that, in the oldest Irish MSS. hitherto printed, we find the same analytic form of speech as is here under consideration. That form of speech is as old, at least, as the times of *Scél mucci Mic Dátho*. So far as the light of manuscripts can guide us, the analytic is not, therefore, the product of a tendency, in that direction, of an older synthetic form. I do not at all forget that the philologist, like the geologist, is accustomed to make very large drafts on the bank of time, and that, behind the line of the oldest manuscript, there lies "a great gulf," where many things may have happened, which are undreamt of in our philosophy. But, while hovering over

the dim wastes of that untried sea, even
the archangels of philology must ply their
" mighty pens " with discretion.

In modern Irish these idioms are still
rife and lively. It were, indeed, not too
much to say that every modern Gaelic
instance of that idiom which is mainly
considered in this chapter, may be taken as
equally illustrative of the living Irish usage.
And the same may, in fact, be said of the
idioms yet remaining to be dealt with, in
the chapters that are to follow.

Parallel usages in Manx are also abundant. As examples we may take the following : *yn thic aym's*=an tigh agam-sa=the
house at me=my house ; *yn cabbyl ayd's*=
an capall agad-sa=the horse at thee=thy
horse ; *yn thie echey*=an tigh aige=the
house at him=his house. In conversa-
tional Gaelic, it may here be observed,
agam, emphatic *agam-sa*=at me=my, is
often shortened into *a'am*, emphatic *a'am-
sa*, which, as spoken, very closely approxi-
mates to the sound of the Manx *aym's*.
Similarly also, *agad*, emphatic *agad-sa*=*a'ad*

=*a'ad-sa*=Manx *ayd's*. On the other
hand the Manx *echy*, *echy*=at him, comes
still nearer the Gaelic *aige*, emphatic *aigesa*,
aigesan, in the form of *eck*.

Even in the popular modern French
some significant remains may still be traced
of the dominancy of what I may now venture to call, at least provisionally, this old
Celtic influence : e.g. *la maison a moi*=the
house at me=my house; and even *ma
maison a moi*=my house at me = my
house.

Similar, but still not exactly parallel, is
an idiom which is often met with in Breton :
e.g. *an dra-ze a zo d'in*=that thing is mine ;
an dra-ze a zo d'id=that thing is thine ;
an dra-ze a zo d'ezhan=that thing is his ;
an dra-ze a zo d'ezhi=that thing is hers ;
te m'oud ket breur d'in=thou art not my
brother.

This Breton preposition, *da*, provincial
de, is difficult to render exactly in another
language. But its meaning is invariably
locative. It comes nearer the English
preposition *to* than *at*. The Gaelic *do*,

before its range of application was limited by a recent decision of the Scotch school of Celtic Grammarians, covered more adequately the ground which this preposition occupies in Breton. But it is closely allied to the use of *aig*, with the verb *tha*, which is now under consideration — an idiom which, through this Breton link, is in fact brought very nearly into line with the similar use of the Latin and Greek dative with the substantive verb : thus, tha tigh agam = est domus mihi = ἐστὶ ὄικος ἐμοί.

And the idiom which thus expresses, through the idea of local proximity, a man's relation to his material property, is also used in a wide but clearly defined province of the sphere of things immaterial. It is, for example, used to express our relation to those of our immaterial properties, or bodily and mental activities, which, like our material property, are still to be conceived of as being in some way subject to our own voluntary control. Thus *tha greim agam ort* = is grip at me on thee = I hold thee ; *tha buaidh agam air* = is power at me on him = I prevail over him; *tha suil agam ris* = is eye at me to him = I expect him; *tha fuath agam da* = is hatred at me to him = I hate him; *tha truas agam ris* = is pity at me to him = I pity him. So also *tha gaol agam* = I love; *tha suim agam* = I regard; *tha speis agam* = I have an attachment. But I cannot say *tha bron agam* = is sorrow at me, when I mean to tell you that I am sorry; nor can I use the words *tha tinneas agam* = is sickness at me, when I mean to tell you that I am sick. It will be seen farther on that these latter visitations, coming upon me involuntarily, and from without, are accordingly connected with me, in Gaelic, by use of the preposition *air* = on.

As parallel usages in Manx to those just discussed, take the following: *ta fys aym* = tha fios agam = is knowledge at me = I know; *ta fys ayd* = tha fios agad = is knowledge at thee = thou knowest; *ta fys echy* = tha fios aige = is knowledge at him = he knows; *ta graih ayd* = tha gradh agad = is love at thee = thou lovest; *ta graih echy* =

tha gradh aige = is love at him = he loves.

Doubly instructive, in this connection, as will be seen in the next chapter, are such phrases as *ta graih aym er* = tha gradh agam air = is love at me on him = I love him.

CHAPTER IV.

THE IDEA OF LOCAL PROXIMITY CONNECTS US
WITH OUR INVOLUNTARY MENTAL AND
BODILY AFFECTIONS : THE USE FOR THAT
PURPOSE OF THE PREPOSITION *AIR*, ON.

LET me try to realise the Celt's first dim,
glimmering consciousness of ethical and religious thought.   The things which are *mine*,
however acquired, are the things which I lay
up unto myself.   They may have become
mine because, hitherto unappropriated by
another, I may have been the first to take
possession of them ; they may have become
mine by conquest; or I may have acquired
them by purchase, or barter, possibly by
inheritance, or even by gift.   Any how,
they are *mine :* I gather them around me ;
and, to keep them in my possession, I keep
them as near me as I can : they are the

things *at* me. But there are things that
come to me, not by act of mine, perhaps
not by wish of mine, but against my will,
and to my grievous loss, hurt, or discom-
fort. They are visitations : it may be sore
inflictions of sickness, suffering, misfortune,
or wrong ; it may be also benign visitations
of relief or gladness. They come to me
from without, and probably from the Unseen. They come always from Above.
They come from a Power, or Powers, to
which I can only submit. They come,
possibly, now from a God, now from a
Devil ; possibly, the ideas of God and
Devil have not yet been clearly differen-
tiated by the rude nomadic Celt.

But while to the primitive Celt his property and voluntary mental states, chosen
and kept by his own act, were *at* him, these
involuntary visitations were *upon* him.
Hunger and thirst; faintness, weariness,
sickness, and sadness; the smallpox, measles,
whooping-cough, the cholera, the plague, if
such in times of primitive simplicity there
were, and death itself, were to his mind,

not abstract conditions, but very real burdens—burdens laid *upon* him, which he
had, in a very literal sense, to undergo, or
carry. Similarly also joy and deliverance
came *upon* him, as very real blessings,
literally conferred by some benign fate or
fairy. And thus, as in the Celtic tongue
a man's relations to his material property,
and to things immaterial, yet his by option
and voluntary control, or at least by con-
sent, are expressed by *aig, at ;* so the relations to men of their involuntary mental
and bodily affections are expressed by *air,
on.* Examples of this idiom might be
multiplied indefinitely : *tha a bhreac orm*
(air mi) = I have the smallpox = is the
smallpox on me ; *bha fuachd ort* (air tu) =
thou wert a-cold = was cold on thee ; *thainig
sgios air'* (air e) = he was a-weary = came
weariness on him ; *tha aoibhneas oirre* (air i)
= she is glad = is gladness on her ; *thainig
saorsa air Seumas* = James was delivered
= came deliverance on James. Sometimes
the *usus loquendi* in regard to this idiom
outruns the strict limits of my definition ;

as, *thainig sgail air mo rosg*=my sight was dimmed=came shade on my sight; or, *chuir e crioch air an obair*=he finished the work=put he end on the work.

Be it again observed, that all these examples would come as readily to the lips of a modern Irishman as to those of a Scotch Highlander. And though the Manxman is not quite so much addicted to the same idiom, yet he too speaks of some at least of these affections as being *orrym*, on me ; *ort*, on thee ; *er*, on him ; *urree*, on her ; *orrin*, on us ; *erriu*, on you ; *orroo*, on them.

Nor is the Welshman a stranger to the same form of speech. All the common ailments of life come *upon* him ; and when he has thus caught an infectious disease, he is, like his Scotch and Irish cousins, *under* it : thus *y mae 'r frech goch arno ef*= the measles are on him ; *y mae 'r frech wen arno ef*=the smallpox is on him ; and, conversely, *y mae dan y frech goch*=he is under the measles ; *y mae dan y frech wen* =he is under the smallpox.

For very distinct examples of this use of *air* in the oldest Irish MSS. one may long search in vain. And such a search is not unlikely to be misleading, as well as fruitless. For the old Irish writers make use of a preposition *ar*, in the different sense of "from" or "against," which, at first sight, a novice is apt to take for the word of which he is in search—e.g., *sochraite de dommanucul arintledaib demna, araslaigthib dualche, arirnechtaib aicnid, arcechnduine miduthrastar dam* = God's army for my defence from the temptations of devils, from the wiles of the wicked, from my nature's passions, and from every man malevolent to me; Zeuss, 2nd edition, p. 624. But still the word, in its modern form, is sometimes to be met with in the oldest Irish writings : e.g., *tesbanat bóill áiriu* = want of members was on them, *dorigeni dia airriu de maid* = what God wrought on them of good (*Ibid.*). It is, however, in the form of *for*, by aspiration *fhor* = 'or, that this preposition usually appears in Old Irish. Under this same form it also appears twice in the two lines of a colophon, which closes the Book of Deir, "certainly as old as the ninth century": see Stokes' *Goidelica*, p. 106, and references there also to Zeuss' *Grammatica Celtica*.

Of the analagous use of *fo*, under, the Old Irish affords many clear examples: thus *fo mám pechto* = under the yoke of sin; *diagmani fo baithis* = let us come under baptism; *retechte fobaithis* = before undergoing baptism; *fonchath* = under battle See Zeuss' *Gram. Celt.*, p. 628.

Observe now the religious significance of this form of Celtic sentence-building It shows already some sense, strong if not yet very clear, of man's subjection to the Unseen. From the great vault above, now radiant with benign light, now clothed with sackcloth and gloom, the dread abode of meteor and thunderbolt, there come upon the children of men at once the blessing and the curse, the reward and the Nemesis, the bloom, on one hand, the bane and blight, on the other, of human life. Coming from Above, these visitations from an unseen source, or from unseen Powers, are *upon us, oirnn:* we have to carry them.

The religious significance of this form of Celtic speech is still further emphasised when we turn to the parallel use, above referred to, of the preposition *fo* = under. The visitation from Above comes *upon us*, and we are therefore *under* it. Piously, therefore, we must *submit*, if it be a visitation of evil, and as bravely as we can, we must *carry* the appointed burden. Joyfully, also, and with grateful heart, if it be a visitation of gladness, or of happy deliverance, must we lift up our eyes to the propitious skies; our yoke is easy and our burden light; let us be strong men, rejoicing to run our race.

The language of Celtic devotion is everywhere alive with the movement of this pregnant linguistic phenomenon. I shall quote but two examples from the Gaelic Psalter. The one is from Psalm xxxiv. 19 (Smith's Version, 1787) :—

Is lionmhor trioblaid agus teinn
thig *air* an fhirean chòir :
Ach *asd* air fad ni Dia nan gràs
a theasairgin fadheoidh.

The other is from Psalm xlii. 11 :—

O m'anam com' a leagadh thu
le diobhail misnich sios ?
Is com' am bheil thu 'n taobh stigh dhiom
fo aimheal is *fo* sgios ?

The spelling of Dr. Smith is here retained.

CHAPTER V.

THE GAEL'S RELATIONS TO MENTAL AND
BODILY STATES, NOT OBVIOUSLY COMING
TO HIM FROM WITHOUT, AND YET NOT
DISTINCTLY VOLUNTARY : THE USE, IN
AN INVERTED FORM, OF THE SAME PRE-
POSITION *AIR, ON.*

WHILE, as has been seen, the Gael has to
bear the incubus of certain bodily and
mental affections, coming to him from without, or perhaps rather from above, there
are also mental and bodily states, more or
less, as would seem, of his own making,
which do not thus, so to speak, bestride
his personality, but which, *vice versa*, he
gets atop of, bestriding them as the rider
does his steed.   Thus, *tha e air mhisg* =

he is drunk = he is on drunkenness (*cf.* American-Irish, he is on the drunk); *tha mi air chrith* = I am a-tremble = I am on trembling; *bha e air at* = he was on swelling, or perhaps *bha e air 'at* = he was on his swelling = he was swollen; *chaidh e air seachran* = he went on wandering = he strayed. Some mental states are put both ways. Thus, *tha e air mhulad*, or *tha mulad air*=he is on sadness, or sadness is on him; *tha e air sgios*, or *tha sgios air*=he is a-weary; *tha e air ocras*, or *tha ocras air* = he is an hungred; *tha e air bhoile*, or *tha boile air* = he is mad.

There is one phrase which, in this con-nection, is specially suggestive : *tha e air chall*=he is on losing=he (or it) is lost. This phrase is of very frequent occurrence in North Highland Gaelic; and by North Highland servant girls in the South the idiom is carried over literally into their attempts to speak English, in a way that is of some linguistic interest. With this large class of my fair countrywomen in

Edinburgh and Glasgow no form of words is more common than " it is on lost," or more usually, and more closely carried over from the Gaelic, "it has gone on lost," or "it went on lost," *chaidh e air chall.* Indeed, so powerful is the linguistic force of this idiom that, among small communities of English - speaking immigrants in the heart of Gaelic-speaking districts of the North Highlands, the phrase "it went on lost," is heard habitually from the lips of persons who never spoke Gaelic. I have heard the phrase hundreds of times among people brought up in Tain, Cromarty, Invergordon, Avoch, and even in Inverness, who were wholly ignorant of the language whose idiom had thus stamped its impress, so vividly and so grotesquely, on their English speech.

Herein the Irish and Scotch Gaelic idioms are identical. But the *usus loquendi* of the Manxman suggests the suspicion that, after all, this lusty shoot from the Gaelic stem may prove to be, not a natural, but an abnormal growth. In

Manx we say *ta mee caillit* = I am lost ; *va mi caillit* = I was lost.   Here, then, so far as the present and past tenses are concerned, we are free from the peculiarities of the idiom now under consideration. But the perfect tense brings up what seems to me to be the normal form, in Manx, of an idiom which, in Irish and Scotch Gaelic, has widened its sphere, while suffering, in the process, some amount of grammatical degeneration.   The perfect tense in Manx is *ta mee er ve caillit*, whose Gaelic equivalent would be *tha mi air bhith caillte* = I am on being lost.   And this *er ve caillit* appears regularly in the Perfect, Plu-perfect, and Future-perfect tenses of the Manx.   But while using this fuller form in the tenses above named, the Manx have also another form, nearer the Gaelic and Irish, which Kelly's *Grammar*, pp. 51, 52, calls "the more elegant form of the verb."   The past and future tenses of *caill*, to lose, are thus "more elegantly" formed in the indicative passive by calling in the help of the irregular verb *goll*, to go, now

represented in Scotch Gaelic only by *doll* =
going, as—

Hie mee er coayl = I went on loss	= I was lost.
Hie oo er coayl = thou wentest on loss = thou wast lost.
Hie eh er coayl = he went on loss	= he was lost.

Now, on the phonetic principles deliber-
ately chosen by the Manx translators of
the Scriptures (see Gill's Introduction to
Kelly's *Manx Grammar*, p. 12), *hie mee* is
the Manx equivalent of the Scotch Gaelic
chaidh mi = I went. Thus *honnick mee* is
at once the exact phonetic scription, and
the scription of the Manx Bible, for the
Scotch Gaelic *chunnaic mi*, I saw. *Heeym*,
I shall see, and *heein*, I might see, are like-
wise the exact phonetic scription, and the
accepted Manx equivalent, for the same
parts of the Scotch Gaelic defective verb
chi, to see. Set forth in tabular form the
past and future tenses passive of the Manx
verb *caill*, to lose, would therefore run
thus—

Manx.	Gaelic.	Lit. English.
Hie mee or coayl	= chaidh mi air chall	= I went on loss.
Hie oo er coayl	= chaidh thu air chall	= thou wentest on loss.
Hie eh er coayl	= chaidh e air chall	= he went on loss.

In this connection, the Future tense is full of interest :—

Manx.	Gaelic.	
H'em er coayl	= theid mi air chall	= I will go on loss.
H'eu er coayl	= theid thu air chall	= thou wilt go on loss.
Hed eh er coayl	= theid e air chall	= he will go on loss.
Hed, *or* hem mayd er coayl	= theid sinn air chall	= we will, &c.
Hed shiu er coayl	= theid sibh air chall	= ye will, &c.
Hed ad er coayl	= theid iad air chall	= they will, &c.

The closer approach here made to Irish than to Scotch Gaelic, and, strange as it may appear, to Sutherland Gaelic rather than to the Gaelic of Argyle, needs only to be noticed in passing.

CHAPTER VI.

CLOSELY allied to the curious linguistic usage just described is another, whereby in Gaelic the same local preposition *air* connects, among other relations, the musician with his instrument, the marksman with his rifle, the painter with his sublime art, the smoker with his pipe, and the toper with his dram. Thus, *tha e math air an fhiodhaill* = he is good on the violin = he is an expert violinist ; *tha e math air a ghunna* = he is good on the gun = he is a good shot ; *tha e trom air an ol*, or *air an deoch* = he is heavy on the drink = he is a sot.

Further instances, in almost endless variety, might easily be introduced, classified, and copiously illustrated, of the multiform uses to which the Gael turns this, perhaps the most versatile of his wonderfully versatile prepositions. At present I must content myself with simply quoting those that follow, leaving the philological expert to classify them for himself, and to subject them to the discriminating tests of his crucible. I merely remark that the relations of super-position or sub-position are common to them all :—*Is òcag orm an duine* = is little on me the man = I dislike, or rather, despise the man; *bheir mi ort a dheanamh* = I will bring on you its doing = I will make you do it; *ghabh e air a ghille* = took he on the lad = he thrashed the lad ; *thog e air* = he lifted on him = he made off ; *thug e am monadh air* = he took the moor on him = he betook himself to the moor = he levanted ; *na gabh ort* = " dinna let on " = " keep dark ; " *c' ainm a th' ort ?* = what name is on thee ? = what is your name ? *Tha Seumas orm* = is James on me = my name

D

is James; *air leth-shuil* = on half eye = blind
of an eye; *air leth-choise* = on half foot =
one-footed; *air leth-laimh* = on half hand =
one-handed; *chuir e an leabhair a leth-
thaobh* = he put the book on one side = he
put the book aside; *air beul-thaobh* = on
mouth side = before; *air cul-thaobh* = on
back-side = behind; *duine air leth* = a man
apart = a man altogether exceptional; *tha
crun agam air Tomas* = is crown at me on
Thomas = Thomas owes me a crown, *cf.*
Welsh, *mae ar Thomas goron i mi* = is on
Thomas crown to me; *tha e air an dall
daorach* = he is blin' fu'; *dean air t-athais*
(*cf.* French, aisé) = " make on your leisure "
= " take it easy."

CHAPTER VII.

THE IDEA OF SETTLED OWNERSHIP, AS DIS-
TINGUISHED FROM THAT OF MERE
ARBITRARY OR CONDITIONAL POSSES-
SION: EXPRESSED BY *LE*, *WITH:* OLD
IRISH *LA.*

ONE way in which, as we have seen,
the Celt became related to his property,
or rather his property to him, was by
his having it near him, and being able
to keep it there. This he expressed
in language by means of the preposition
aig, *at.* What we call his property may
have been captured by violence, and may
have been retained by force. Or it may
have been left under his charge for a season
by a man of stronger arms who might

return and take it again. He could never be sure that, at any time, a stronger than he should not come and spoil him of his goods. There is, however, another way (shall I say of later development among the Celts?) in which property, or rather the rightful possession of property, is brought into verbal relation to its owner. This is by use of the preposition *le, with*. In this way my property is represented as, not merely *at me, agam*, but *with me, leam* —resting, abiding with me — mine with more or less of a conscious sense of right, and with the feeling of guaranteed security, which, to the dawning moral sense, is bred of the ideas of right and settled ownership. Without at all pretending to dogmatise on the subject, it appears to me that there can be traced in the Celtic tongues a good linguistic basis, at least for suggesting such a differentiation of the idea, on the one hand, of property held arbitrarily and con- ditionally, and the idea, on the other hand, of property, not so much *held*, as possessed and enjoyed, by virtue of the legal or ethical right of acknowledged ownership. To say that the idea of this distinction is always consciously observed in the common use of the Celtic or any other tongues, would be absurd. But there can be no doubt that there is, as has been said, a sufficient basis for the clear suggestion of such a distinction. "Co leis an damh donn," I once said, in sauntering along the stalls of the Highland Society's great Cattle Show, to a brawny Highlander, stretched at full length on the straw beside a magnificent Highland bull, to which the first prize had just been awarded. "Tha e leamsa," proudly and promptly replied the Highlander, whom I afterwards found to be the celebrated Stewart of Duntuilm, in the Isle of Skye. His herdsman, or his grieve, could not use the same words. You might say to either of them "is math am beathach a th' agad," but only the owner could say "is leams' e" = "he is with me = "he is mine." In like manner, and observing the same distinction, you could say to the cashier of a bank, as you saw him shovelling about his golden sovereigns with a copper scoop, " tha moran airgiod *agad*, ach cha *leats'* a bheag dheth " = " is 'much money *at thee*, but not *with thee* is little of it " = " you have charge of much money, but none of it is your own." That the distinction between *agam* = at me, and *leam* = with me, is always so clear as in the cases here put, cannot of course be asserted. But these cases will suffice to show that the distinction indicated in this chapter is real, and that it is readily understood.

Joyce, in his admirable little grammar of modern Irish for the use of schools, has an apposite illustration of the main distinction which is suggested in this chapter : *ta airgead go leor agad, acht ní leat féin é* = thou hast plenty of money, but it does not belong to thyself.

There is a large class of cases, in which by means of this preposition, *le* = with, we may be said to express such preferences or conclusions as, professedly at least, are the result of some measure of thought and calm reflection. Thus, *is fearr leam an t-each so* = is better with me this horse = I prefer this horse : however the matter may be with others, for my part, speaking and judging for myself, and after duly weighing every element of the comparison, I conclude that this is, at least for me, the better horse of the two. Similarly also may be classified such examples as *is annsa leam* = is more dear with me = I prefer; *is coma leam* = is indifferent with me = I don't care for; *is caomh leam e* = is lovely with me he = I like him; *is bochd leat* = is poor with thee = it is a pity, in your view; *is truagh leinn* = is sad with us = we regret it; *is cuimhne leo* = is remembrance with them = they remember it; *'nochd is trom leam mo chridhe* = to-night is heavy with me my heart; *tha e leam, leat* = he is with thee, with me = he is a trimmer.

The following examples in Old Irish are taken from Windisch's *Irische Texte : is lat in fer*, p. 224; *bád maith lim-sa*, p. 210; (*is*) *cumma lem*, p. 140; *is maith lind*, p. 103.

From the examples here given it would

seem as if to the Celtic mind a man's views and opinions, his likings and dislikes, are his—*with* him, as his inalienable right— just as much, and in the same way, as the property of which he is the undoubted owner. His wilder passions, such as rage and fear, are *on* him, like madness or the plague: some of them, like hatred and malice, are *at* him, like the spoils of rapine and violence. But, on the other hand, and, probably, amid more humane sur- roundings, his cooler judgments, his deli- berate opinions, his reasonable preferences, his rational likings and dislikes, even his childish prejudices, are *with* him, like those peaceful fruits of industry, and these simple trinkets so dear to his childish tastes, which are his by virtue of law and settled right. Is it too much to suggest that the one idiom originated amid deeds of violence, and under the shadow of gloomy supersti- tions, while the other was the product of brighter, because more peaceful, times?

CHAPTER VIII.

THE behaviour in Gaelic sentence-building
of the preposition *ann*, in, usually with the
possessive pronoun, introduces us to certain
very remarkable philological problems,
which it is not easy to solve. Such phrases
as *an diugh*=to-day, *an nochd*=to-night,
an dé=yesterday, may be summarily dis-
posed of. For the *an* here is not at all a
preposition, as some seem to fancy. It is
evidently the article, as witness the equivalent Scoto-Gaelic phrases, " the day "=to-

day, " the nicht "= to-night, " he cam' hame
the day and leaves the nicht "= he came
home to-day and leaves to-night, " he gaes
awa' the morn's mornin' " = he goes away
to-morrow morning. The curious and
perplexing idiom now under consideration
is entirely different from this. It is glanced
at by Stewart in his *Gaelic Grammar*, 2nd
edition, pp. 136, 137, where he makes some
show of explaining it. That no injustice
may be done to this, the ablest of all our
Scotch Gaelic grammarians, I shall quote
here all that he has written on the subject.

Under the heading, *ann, ann an, anns*,
he gives the following as one of three
several definitions :—" Denoting existence :
ta abhainn ann, there is a river, Ps. xlvi. 4
metr, *nach bithinn ann ni's mò*, that I should
not be any more : *b' fhearr a bhi marbh na
ann'*, it were better to be dead than to be
alive : *ciod a th' ann?* what is it ? *is mise
th' ann*, it is I : *mar gu b' ann*, as it were :
tha e 'n a dhuine ionraic, he is a just man :
tha i 'n a bantraich, she is a widow." And
in a footnote to this paragraph Stewart

adds, "this use of the preposition *ann* in conjunction with the possessive pronoun, is nearly akin to that of the Hebrew ל (for), in such expressions as these; He made me (for) a father to Pharaoh, and (for) lord of all his house, *rinn e mi 'n am athair do Pharaoh, agus 'n am thighearn os ccann a thighe uile*, Gen. xlv. 8. Thou hast taken the wife of Uriah to be (for) thy wife, *ghabh thu bean Uriah gu bhi 'n a mnaoi dhuit fein*, 2 Sam. xii. 10."

But Dr. Stewart entirely evades the real difficulty of his own quotations. Taken literally, *bha e 'n a dhuine ionraic* = was he in his man just; and *ghabh thu bean Uriah gu bhi 'na mnaoi dhuit fein* = taken hast thou (the) wife of Uriah to be in her woman to thyself. The real question is, how are we to explain the use of the preposition and possessive pronoun in this very peculiar idiom? And it appears to me that the idiom is one which, to the philologist, is fraught with a depth of interest such as can be measured only by its undoubted obscurity. I must, however, frankly confess my inability, thus far, to offer any explanation which meets all the requirements of this curious philological puzzle. That curious puzzle I have turned over, and turned about, scanning it as narrowly as I could, in every possible light, and from every conceivable point of view. I have examined it, and cross-examined it, philologically, and I have tried to scrutinise its history in every conceivable way. But I have not been able satisfactorily to get at the true story of its birth and growth. Perhaps, if it could speak, its answer would be none other than the answer of Canning's knife-grinder : " Story ? God bless you, I have none to tell, sir." For there are many other curious things than Topsies, that " growed " no one knows how. That may be so. And yet I cannot believe that so it is. I have elaborated several theories, each of which seemed, for a time, to account for all the multiform developments of this paradoxical idiom. But there is no theory that, after deliberate, critical consideration, I can venture to present as an adequate solution of the difficulty. One suggestion only I will here presume to offer. It is that the modern Gaelic language, and especially colloquial Gaelic, as opposed to the book-Gaelic of scholars, does not take kindly to the use of abstract words. Indeed it may almost be said, that Nature does not more heartily abhor a vacuum, than the colloquial speech of the modern Highlander abhors the abstract. The genuine, unsophisticated Gael of the Scottish Highlands would never dream of saying, in an abstract way, *tha min daor, ach tha sgadan saor*=meal is dear, but herring is cheap. He would say, *tha a mhin daor, ach tha an sgadan saor*=the meal is dear, but the herring is cheap. Now, in whatever way the philologist may be able ultimately to solve the difficulties of the curious idiom here under consideration, I believe that this Celtic abhorrence of the abstract will be found to form a notable element in the solution. The Gael does not rest satisfied with simply saying, of his friend, that he is angelic, and of his enemy, that he is devilish. Inspired by the " space " idea which regulates all his attempts at sentence-building, he rather puts it that the one *is in his angel*, and the other *in his devil.*

With this suggestion, I leave the sphere of theory, and turn to facts, the only basis on which theories can ever be profitably reared.

I propose, therefore, now (1) to show, as clearly as I can, wherein the principle of this idiom consists, and (2) to classify and exemplify its main varieties.

The question *ciod a th' ann ?* is translated by Stewart as " what is it ? " This, however, is not a translation, but a paraphrase. Written without contraction the question is *ciod a tha ann?* and the translation is " what which is in it ? " In like manner, Stewart's answer to this question, *is mise th' ann,* would, if written at length, be *is mise a tha ann*=it is I that is in it. And it is significant that the colloquial English of districts in which Gaelic was long the dominant language, still answers exactly to this idiom. In such districts the great bulk of the people would say, not "who is there?" but "who is in it?" And the answer would be, not "it is I," but "it's me that's in it." This strong "*local* colour" —this seemingly ridiculous exaggeration of the "space idea"—is of the very essence of the idiom; and that it is so must be borne clearly in mind all through this and the following chapters.

Thus *tha e 'n a chealgair* = he is in his cheat, is the usual phrase, by means of which in Gaelic you declare that a man is a cheat. But, in emphatic speech, I have often heard the idiom more fully expressed, as *tha e ann a chealgair.* Or if you wish to speak even more strongly, you can say *tha e ann a fhior chealgair* = he is in his real cheat = he is an arrant rogue. It will be seen that, up to this point, the possessive pronoun, *a*, plays in this idiom a part as indispensable as the preposition *ann*, in. But by turning your statement into the negative form, you can both drop the possessive pronoun, and at the same time greatly intensify your cacology. To say

cha 'n eil ann ach am fior chrochair = there
is not in him but the true gallows-man,
affords a vent for the relief of one's pent-
up historical conscience, such as might well
send a pang of envy to the heart of the
senior wrangler of Billingsgate.

CHAPTER IX.

THE IDEA OF "SPACE" RELATION, AS EX-
PRESSED BY THE PREPOSITION *ANN*, IN :
LEADING VARIETIES OF THIS IDIOM
CLASSIFIED AND EXEMPLIFIED.

HAVING seen that the essential element of
this idiom is the "space idea" expressed
by the preposition, *ann*, in, I proceed now
to classify and illustrate the main varieties
which it presents in the living speech of
the Highlander.

1. This idiom covers the whole ground
occupied by a man's trade or profession.

If you ask a Highland boy what his
father works at for a living, he will answer
you, in this idiom, *tha e 'n a shaor*=he is
in his carpenter, *tha e 'n a mhaor*=he is in

E

his officer, *tha e 'n a thaillear*=he is in his tailor, and so on, as the case may be. A precocious urchin, who "speaks like a book," may sometimes say *is saor e*=is carpenter he, *is maor e*=is officer he, *is taillear e*=is tailor he. But ninety answers in the hundred would be as I have first put it. Similarly we say, *tha e 'n a shagart*= he is in his priest, *tha e 'n a mhinistear*= he is in his minister, *tha e 'n a bhreitheamh* =he is in his judge.

2. The idiom extends to one's outward attitudes : *tha e 'n a sheasamh*=he is in his standing=he stands, *tha e 'n a dhuisg*=he is in his waking=he is awake, *tha e 'n a chadal*=he is in his sleep=he sleeps, *tha e 'n a thamh*=he is in his resting=he rests, *tha e 'n a laidhe*=he is in his reclining=he reclines, *tha e 'n a shlainte*=he is in his health=he is well (*cf.* English, he is in health), and we even say *tha e 'n a ruith* =he is in his running=he runs, *tha e 'n a chabhaig*=he is in his hurry=he hurries.

3. The idiom under consideration covers also the whole field of a man's character

and reputation : *tha e 'n a fhircan* = he is in his true one = he is a just man, *tha e 'n a ghaisgcach* = he is in his hero = he is a hero, *tha e 'n a sgoilear* = he is in his scholar = he is a learned man, *tha e 'n a dhuine uasal* = he is his man honourable = he is a gentle-man, *tha i 'n a bean shunndach* = she is in her woman healthily-happy = she is a well-conditioned, joyous woman. Similarly also we say *tha e 'n a bhreugaire* = he is in his liar = he is a liar, *tha e 'n a ghealtair* = he is in his coward, *cha 'n 'cil ann ach burraidh* = there is not in him but a blockhead, *cha 'n 'cil ann ach an Turcach* = there is not in him but the Turk.

4. Personal accidents of extraction, sex, country, and such like, find expression in Gaelic by means of the same idiom : *tha 'n leanabh 'n a ghille* = the child is in his boy = the child is a boy, *tha am paisde 'n a nighean* = the child is in her daughter = the child is a girl, *tha e 'n a leanabh diolain* = he is in his child illegitimate (of recom-pense ?) = he is a bastard. Similarly also, we say *tha e 'n a choigreach* = he is in his

stranger = he is a stranger, *tha e 'n a Sha-sunnach*, or, *is e Sasunnach a th' ann* = he is in his Englishman, or, it is an English-man that is in him, or, yet again, *cha 'n 'eil ann ach Sasunnach* = there is not in him but an Englishman.

5. Personal attributes, of which, in English, we usually conceive as being, more or less, of the nature of abstractions, are in Gaelic, through this idiom, made emphatically concrete to the individual : thus, *tha e 'n a leth-chiallach* = he is in his half-witted one = he is half-witted, *tha e 'n a thruaghan* = he is in his miserable one = he is miserable, *tha e 'n a amadan* = he is in his fool = he is foolish. A better definition, perhaps, of this variety of the idiom, than that given above, is that, converting the abjective descriptive of a man's abstract condition into a personal noun, it takes that personal noun and, so to speak, plants the man in the heart of it. Thus, while, as in English, we say *tha an duine balbh* = the man is dumb, yet, by means of this idiom, we concrete and animate the man's abstract

quality of dumbness, and, planting him in the heart of our creation, we say, *tha an duine 'n a bhalbhan* = the man is in his dumb one, or as, owning the influence of this Gaelic idiom, we say in vulgar Scotch, he is a "dummie." In like manner, when we speak of a man as being alone, we say *tha e 'n a aon-fhear* = he is in his one-man, and when we speak of his being silent, we say *tha e 'n a thosd* = he is in his silence.

6. The condition to which persons or things tend, or which, as the result of an antecedent tendency, they have already reached, is often expressed in the same way: *tha e air fas 'n a shean duine* = he has grown in(to) his old man = he has grown old, *theid a chlach-mhuilcann 'n a smurach* = the millstone will go into its dust = the millstone will be smashed, *chaidh an tigh 'n a theine* = the house went in its fire, *chaidh an teine 'n a smal* = the fire went in its embers, *nithear an tir 'n a fhasach* = the land will be made in its wilderness = the land will be laid waste, *nithear am fasach*

'n a linne uisge=the wilderness will be made in its pool of water.

Through all the varied uses of this idiom, among much that is but of secondary interest, my primary position will not, I hope, be forgotten. We have seen that the relation, which connects men and things with a very large portion of their conditions and belongings, is the relation of *locality*— the "space" relation. As things and states were seen to affect us and to become related to us, because they were *at* us, or *on* us, or *with* us, so now, *vice versa*, things and states affect us and become related to us, all the more, because we are *in* them. My virtue or vice, my courage or cowardice, my habits and stated avocations, my physical, mental, and moral attitudes, are no longer mere accidents of my personality. They are grafted, as living branches into the tree of my personality; or rather my personality is merged in them. What I am to myself and to the world, my worth or worthlessness, is just what they make me, and enable me to do in the way of good or evil, of hurt or help unto the children of men. Thus does word-history repeat itself, just as does the history of men, of races, and of nations. The Red Indian and the perfect English gentleman have much in common. I am not thinking now of their common share in our common humanity, but of certain moral qualities common to the one, as Red Indian, and to the other, as perfect English gentleman. Both alike have tacitly agreed to suppress emotion : they show no sign of feeling or surprise, in circumstances which to ordinary mortals are largely productive of both. They are separated by a gulf, social and ethnical, which is wider and deeper than the Atlantic; but herein they are at one. And, even so, the rude nomadic Celt's first efforts to depict in words the moral worth or demerit of himself and others are at one with the carefully elaborated word-pictures, in the same line, of the most polished of modern poets.

Worth makes the man, and want of it the fellow ;
The rest is all but leather and prunello.

www.ingramcontent.com/pod-product-compliance
Lightning Source LLC
Chambersburg PA
CBHW021524270326
41930CB00008B/1088